GOODBYE MOM

Ann (Klassen) Brown

 FriesenPress

Suite 300 - 990 Fort St
Victoria, BC, V8V 3K2
Canada

www.friesenpress.com

ISBN
978-1-5255-0449-5 (Hardcover)
978-1-5255-0450-1 (Paperback)
978-1-5255-0451-8 (eBook)

1. BIOGRAPHY & AUTOBIOGRAPHY

Distributed to the trade by The Ingram Book Company

Dear Pat:

I hope you enjoy reading my book.

Keep smiling!

:)

Your friend Ann.

ABrown

04/09/19

This book is dedicated to my beautiful family who have been my joy in life. Special thanks to my wonderful husband Fred, whose love and support has made writing this book, possible.

Table of Contents

Preface

THE VILLAGE BLACKSMITH

Under the spreading chestnut tree
The village smithy stands;
The smith, a mighty man is he,
With large and sinewy hands;
And the muscles of his brawny arms
Are strong as iron bands.

His hair is crisp, and black, and long,
His face is like the tan;
His brow is wet with honest sweat,
He earns whate'er he can,
And looks the whole world in the face,
For he owes not any man.

Week in, week out, from morn till night,
You can hear his bellows blow;
You can hear him swing his heavy sledge
With measured beat and slow,
Like a sexton ringing the village bell,
When the evening sun is low.

And children coming home from school
Look in at the open door;
They love to see the flaming forge,
And hear the bellows roar,
And watch the burning sparks that fly
Like chaff from a threshing-floor.

He goes on Sunday to the church,
And sits among his boys;
He hears the parson pray and preach,
He hears his daughter's voice
Singing in the village choir,
And it makes his heart rejoice.

It sounds to him like her mother's voice
Singing in Paradise!
He needs must think of her once more,
How in the grave she lies;
And with his hard, rough hand he wipes
A tear out of his eyes.

Toiling, rejoicing, sorrowing,
Onward through life he goes;
Each morning sees some task begin,
Each evening sees it close;
Something attempted, something done,
Has earned a night's repose.

Thanks, thanks to thee, my worthy friend.
For the lesson thou hast taught!
Thus at the flaming forge of life
Our fortunes must be wrought;
Thus on its sounding anvil shaped
Each burning deed and thought!

Henry Wadsworth Longfellow. 1807-1882

I believe that this poem was written about my father. Even if Longfellow didn't know my Dad, it is uncanny how he describes him perfectly. We did live in a village, he didn't owe money to anyone, on Sundays in our church the boys and men sat on one side and the girls and women sat on the other side, I sang in the choir, Mom was in a grave and Dad worked very hard from morning until dusk. The only difference in his description was that although Dad did have black hair, it was never long.

This is the story of my childhood and the emphasis is on my dad. It was he, who taught me compassion, love and respect for others. The many experiences of my childhood, good and bad, helped to make me the person I am today. With my belief in God and the strength and love of my dad, I learned to be strong to survive the things that life dealt to me. I will be forever grateful to him for all he sacrificed to keep my sister and me together through what must have been a very hard and painful time for him. He had no one to share things with. Helen and I had each other. Now my parents and siblings are all together again renewing all the past memories. Till we meet again!

CHAPTER I
One Never Knows

Many years ago, there lived a blacksmith in a small village on the prairies. This blacksmith had a sickly wife and six healthy, robust children.

This blacksmith worked hard from dusk to dawn, just as Tennyson's blacksmith had. It was a struggle to make ends meet as blacksmithing was not a very profitable occupation.

This family was happy but sometimes you wouldn't know it as the three boys could fight like cats and dogs. The two youngest girls fought sometimes but with them, they fought more like kittens and puppies.

The everyday humdrum of their lives was abruptly put to a halt as their sickly mother closed her eyes for the last time and went to join her own mother who had passed away many years ago.

The oldest three children were already away from home, so that left a brokenhearted father, the youngest son and two young girls to fend for themselves.

As many others have encountered, this family began a new, lonely life as they continued to try to live their lives as normal as possible but at times seemed anything but normal.

As I have said blacksmithing was not a very profitable occupation. So imagine our surprise when one day, Dad handed Helen and I each a dollar! If Dad ever gave us money to spend it was usually five cents. We didn't complain because you could buy quite a lot for five cents in those days. But a whole dollar...for each of us! We could hardly believe this, and before he had a chance to change his mind, Helen and I ran to the cafe at the hotel. We bought sundaes, pop, chocolate bars and gum and as we were eating them, suddenly it dawned on me. Tomorrow was Father's Day! He gave us the money so we could buy him a Father's Day gift. We couldn't give back the sundaes, almost empty pop, and partly eaten chocolate bars or opened up gum. We were sick, not only from eating all those delicious treats, but to think now we had nothing to give to Dad. Then a bright idea came to me. We went to grocery store where we knew the owner real well. I told him what we had done and asked if we could buy something on credit and pay him back when we had enough babysitting money. He agreed, so we bought some beautiful handkerchiefs in a box and a very nice card. Dad was very happy with the gift and card and he never did find out how greedy his daughters had been.

Such was one of our adventures, if you can call it such, in our life without a mother and with a Dad who was in new territory.

Chapter 2
"Blacksmith Bill"

The blacksmith - William or "Blacksmith Bill" Klassen as he was also known - was born in Romanofky, Russia on September 26, 1894. He emigrated to Canada in 1904 with his parents and their six children, besides himself, taking up a homestead two miles south of Herbert.

My dad, "Blacksmith Bill

He had three siblings that were born at Herbert, Saskatchewan. From there he moved to Clarkboro where he worked for a well drilling outfit and also worked in the general store. While living in Clarkboro he met my mother Annie Matthies of Rabbit Lake. Annie was not married but had a beautiful little daughter, Lydia. He fell in love with both of them. Mom and Dad were married on July 22, 1928.

Dad and Mom on their wedding day

Dad started a blacksmith shop in Clarkboro. Before he knew it, his business had expanded to a wide area. In 1933 he moved his shop to Aberdeen where he built a house.

He added on to it as his family grew. He was as honest as the day was long and worked hard from dawn to dusk, sharpening ploughshares, shoeing horses and many other things that the people in the community required him to do. We found out after he passed away, there were some well to do people that never paid up the bills they owed him. We never asked them for the money either. We just hope that their money made them happier than making life easier for Dad. Gentle, kind to a fault.

Dad was a very good father and loved us children dearly. Every night, before going to bed, Helen and I would kneel down with our hands folded on Dad's knee and heads bowed to say our goodnight prayer. Then with a kiss on the top of our heads from Dad and a kiss from Mom, off to bed we went, feeling safe and loved. We always said the prayer in German but a close translation would be;

I am little,
My heart is clean,
No one lives in it
But Jesus alone.

Another song I remember Dad singing to us in the morning when we were small was:

Good morning merry sunshine,
How did you wake so soon?
You scared away the little stars
And shone away the moon.
I saw you go to bed last night
Before I ceased my praying.
How did you get way over there,
And where have you been staying?

When some of us were struck down with scarlet fever, we were quarantined. I was one of them. Mom pulled all the blinds down tightly so we would not be subjected to any bright light. For the full length of the quarantine, we never saw Dad. He set up a cot in the blacksmith shop and mom would make his meals and set them outside on the step. Dad would pick them up, eat them and then return the dishes to the doorstep for Mom to pick up and wash. We really missed Dad (or Daddy as we called him) during this time. How he must have missed us too!

During the years that Dad was a business man in the community, he served some time as Mayor. While Mayor he had a pleasant surprise when he received a letter from the Mayor of Aberdeen, Scotland. The two of them wrote back and forth for some years after that. Dad gave Helen and me some of these interesting letters to read.

The biggest honour Dad was ever given was by the Bank Manager, Hugh Goudie. I was an employee at the time when Mr Goudie had to leave town for a couple of days. He asked Dad if he would come in during his absence to sit at the desk during work hours for added security. I was so proud of him as he put on his suit, white shirt and tie and sat and visited with the customers as they came in. A small thing for Mr Goudie, but a huge honour for a retired blacksmith. He was very proud that Helen and I both worked for the Bank after graduating. He would have been so proud to know that Dale made banking his successful life career.

Dad always stressed to us that he did not want his children to "shovel shit for some farmer," or "wash shitty diapers for someone else." Bill and Corney attended Normal School in Saskatoon. Then they both taught in rural communities in Saskatchewan before they each chose different careers. Bill as a Conservation Officer and Corney as a member of the Calgary City Police Force. Helen and I both worked at the local bank until we were married. Before she married, Lydia picked fruit in British Columbia in the summers and helped out at home in the winters. John went from job to job for the rest of his life that never consisted of "shovelling shit for a farmer." So Dad's wish for us came true.

When Mom died in 1949, Dad was a very lonely man. I remember him standing at the north window (the cemetery was north of us) and seeing the tears fall down his cheeks. After Mom passed away, one of her sisters wanted Dad to let Helen and I live with them. They had two boys. Dad told her that he had already lost his wife and he would not lose his girls too. We were so glad he said that because we didn't want to leave him. Besides, one summer when mom was sick, Helen and I went to their place for a week. Whenever the two boys fought, they would have to kneel down and pray for God's forgiveness. Helen and I got along better that week than we ever had before or after. We did not want to live like that, besides, Helen and I fought a lot and we would have had very sore knees before long. But we did love our Aunt and it was very good of her to even consider taking us in. After that whenever we misbehaved and Dad threatened to send us to Reform School, we didn't really pay much attention, but when he threatened to send us to our Aunt's, we toed the line very carefully.

Dad had a battle with colon cancer for many years before finally succumbing to it. Once, when he came back from a visit to British Columbia earlier than we had expected, he was very upset with Helen and me for not having the house clean. He said, "You know I have cancer!" I immediately broke down and cried and cried. I couldn't stand the thought of Helen and I being all alone. When he got me settled down, he explained that he was going to take radiation treatments. He even showed us the ink marks on his stomach where they were going to do the radiation. He got through those treatments very well.

Dad was a very avid reader. He built himself a book case. It was almost as tall as the ceiling, probably about five feet wide and a foot deep. It had two doors on it. Inside, it was filled with books, books, and more books. The bottom two shelves were occupied by Encyclopedias and The Books Of Knowledge. Helen and I spent hours reading The Books of Knowledge. They were filled with the most fabulous information about whatever you wanted to know and How To Do Projects of all kinds. Helen and I were both avid readers as well, although as I began raising children and living on a busy farm, my reading went by the wayside. Helen read many, many books while her children were at home and after they grew up and left home. When she lived in Saskatoon, she would bring a shopping bag full of books home from the library and a week later she would return them and bring back another shopping bag full. A trait we both inherited from our Dad.

Dad really enjoyed fishing so we spent most summer Sunday afternoons at the South Saskatchewan River near Clarkboro. Helen and I played while he fished. Then he was kind enough to teach me how to scale and clean the fish. Guess I must have been a good learner as that was my job from there on in. Because of his love for the quiet and calmness of fishing, when he retired in 1963, Dad enjoyed visiting Helen and Frank at Canoe Narrows and Bill and Mildred, who lived in various places in the north. He enjoyed many, many hours of fishing.

Dad fishing

It was such a treat for him to catch other fish than the suckers he caught in the Saskatchewan River.

Dad was always very good to us children and if we needed discipline, that was his area to look after. As he had pounded out many ploughshares with a sledge hammer, his hands were very strong. A couple of whacks (that was usually the extent of it) and he got across what behaving meant. I don't recall any of us girls getting punished this way but my three brothers were a different story. They fought worse than cats and dogs at times.

Dad's garden was the envy of many in Aberdeen. He planted three big trees in the back yard. On the east side of the house were enormous ferns and along the fence were raspberries. He tried to plant strawberries but never had much luck with them. In the garden to the north of the house he had plum trees, gooseberry bushes and the most beautiful apple tree. It was under this tree that I did most of my studying in the summer. There wasn't a weed on his property and I loved lying under the apple tree on my back and looking up to see what pictures I could find in the clouds.

Dad's trees in winter

You may remember the story of when your Dad (Grandpa) and I got engaged. We were so excited and rushed in to tell him and show him my ring. He was just furious. Never said anything and wouldn't even look at us. After your Dad (Grandpa) left to go back to Central Butte, I asked Dad why he was so upset. He said, "You are my daughter and he should have asked for your hand in marriage. Besides," he replied, "for all I know, he could be Irish!!" I had no idea what he had against the Irish. He was very happy to know that his daughter was marrying a Mennonite.

In 1963, Dad was forced to retire from the blacksmith shop due to ill health. His remaining years were spent fishing in the Northern Lakes, travelling, visiting his family, tending his excellent garden, flowers and fruit trees and playing "schmeer" at the back of the butcher shop with his friends.

Dad's brother Pete Klassen, who had been working for a rancher at Herbert for many years, retired and decided he wanted to spend the rest of his years with his dear brother. So in the spring of 1961 he came to Aberdeen. There he made his home with dad until his sudden passing on March 29, 1966 at the age of sixty -four years. Dad and Uncle Pete got along just great. They were always looking out for each other. All of us and our children adored Uncle Pete.

Uncle Pete

He had always lived at Herbert and had been a cowboy for most of his lifetime. His employer had passed away suddenly and his two sons were running the ranch. They were doing things that Uncle Pete disagreed with so he quietly packed up and moved on. He had been a very tall man in his younger years but now was quite stooped. But to us he had not only been tall in stature but also was tall in love, gentleness and kindness. Dad was heartbroken after he passed away. He buried him in the family plot in the Aberdeen Cemetery.

Dad suffered again with colon cancer for a few years and at last was reunited with his dear wife on July 18, 1973 at the age seventy-nine. He was a good husband, father, grandfather, brother, uncle and friend. He rests in the Aberdeen Cemetery between his beloved wife and his special brother Pete.

CHAPTER 3
Gentle, Sweet Mother O'Mine

Annie Matthies was a kind and gentle woman that was loved by all. She was born in Rosenhof, South Russia on November 30, 1902. As a child, her life was not easy as she was the oldest of a family of nine children and two step children. Her mother Susanna (Schmidt) passed away at the age of forty-two leaving children from the age of one to sixteen years for Mom, who was nineteen years old, to look after and feed. A year later Grandpa remarried a widow Amalia Isaak, who had two children ages, eleven and thirteen. So Mom was kept very busy at home helping out with ten children aged one to seventeen years old.

Mom and her mother Susanna and the family.
Mom is first on the left row at the back

Mom's Dad, Grandpa Matthies was a school teacher and when World War I began in 1915, Grandpa Matthies was called to service in the Caucasus Russian Turkish war zone. He was enlisted as an aide to the doctors and hospital units. We would now call it the Red Cross. The war ended in 1917 and Grandpa Matthies went back to teaching.

During the war, life was very hard for the people in that area. Many men were shot or exiled to Siberia, and women were raped. When the soldiers came around, Grandma Matthies hid all the girls in the attic to keep them safe. There was nothing to eat in the attic but I remember Mom telling us that there was an old cow hide up there. That is what they chewed on. As it was not too tightly built up there, there was also some snow for them to melt in their mouths to survive. They all did survive.

Later on, Mom met a Russian soldier that she fell in love with. Grandpa told her they were emigrating to Canada. But I imagine that Mom was tired of being the oldest and always looking after little ones so she wanted to marry this soldier and remain in Russia. Grandpa was very much against this as he did not want to leave his beloved daughter behind when they left. Even when Mom told him she was pregnant with the soldiers child, Grandpa would not change his mind. I imagine the travel across the ocean in a ship must have been very difficult for her.

The family immigrated to Canada in 1925. Then they moved to Great Deer Saskatchewan and then on to Rabbit Lake where they settled their homestead. After Mom's beautiful daughter was born, Grandma offered to look after her so Mom could go out and get a job to help make ends meet in this new country. She went to work at a Doukabor colony where she looked after the small children.

As the years passed and the children all had moved to make homes of their own, Grandpa and Grandma decided it was time to leave the farm. Aunt Helen, Aunt Katheryne and Uncle John had previously moved to British Columbia, so, Grandma and Grandpa bought a small acreage at Sardis, British Columbia.

Mom missed them very, very much. Dad and Mom made a trip to visit them in their new home.

Dad and Mom at Sardis, British Columbia

As Mom's health was failing, it was the only trip they made to see them. Mom wrote many letters to them on whatever paper she could find. In those days they didn't have such things as Iphones, Ipad, Skype, Internet, Face Time (which we take for granted these days) as they were not yet invented. And most certainly not every house had a telephone, and our house was no exception.

After Grandpa Matthies passed away, Aunt Helen sent me some letters that Mom had written to Grandpa and Grandma. Most of these letters are written in German Script. So far I have not been able to find someone to translate them for me, but from what I have gathered from what little I could decipher, Mom loved Grandpa and Grandma very much and they returned her love.

As a wife and mother, life again was not an easy one as she had six children that she had to tend to. On meagre supplies, she cooked and baked for her brood and always had extra for company, or if someone in the community was in need. She cared for her little ones when they were sick and never complained. She spent many hours at the treadle sewing machine resewing clothes given to her by some of her more fortunate neighbours. I remember sitting and playing on the floor beside the sewing machine while she sang and sewed her beautiful creations.

Helen and me in our new coats that Mom sewed

With her tailoring talent, her six children were as well dressed as the "bankers children."

At this point I must explain what I mean by the "banker's children." In those days the banker in the community was most highly respected by almost everyone. My Dad was no exception. The bankers children were always well dressed. So he was very proud of Mom's skills, although we didn't have much money, no one could look down on us for the way we were dressed.

I don't have a lot of memories of Mom, but I treasure the ones I have.

Mom with me hiding in her skirts

The smell of her...now I know it was a body odour but to me it smelled good and it was her. The beautiful cotton dresses she sewed for herself. The day she went downtown and came home with her hair permed. She was giggling She thought it was too fuzzy but we thought she was just beautiful. I will never forget the smell of baking when we came home from school. Anytime someone passed away in the community, Mom somehow found enough to bake some buns for them.

She was always helping other people in the community. In 1945 - 46 a close friend had a nervous breakdown and ended up in the hospital. Mom took in their little baby and looked after him for some months until the baby's mother could come home and take care of him, herself. She already had a large houseful but there was always room for another. He slept in a pulled out dresser drawer. Helen and I just loved playing with him.

Mom had a beautiful alto voice. One of my earliest memories were sitting on her lap in church and listening to her beautiful voice singing the hymns she loved so well. She often sang at home while working and sewing.

Saturdays and Sundays were special in our house. On Saturday Mom would bake and cook for the following day. The house smelled so good!! I think that was the one of the things I really missed after she got sick and passed away. She tried to teach me how to bake bread and buns, but I wasn't even twelve yet. Then on Sunday, after church, we would have company come in for dinner and to spend the day, or we would go visit at friends that lived on a farm. What fun!!

One of the families we visited often was that of Peter Koops. He was the minister in the church. His wife made the BEST cream puffs I have ever eaten. She made them while we were there. They had milk cows, and she whipped real cream (with our help) to put inside them. As it happened, Auntie Hilda's husband Ben was a nephew of Peter Koops.

There was another farm family that stays in my memory. They had two girls and three boys. The boys were all mentally challenged. The oldest was much so. The other two were more normal. Mom always reminded us, "Do not make fun of the boys. They can't help being the way they are." We had a lot of fun playing in their pasture. There were a lot of clumps of trees and we named each one and had a great time with our lively imaginations.

When I was probably seven or so, Dad built a small barn and bought a milk cow. Friends of ours told Mom she could put the cow in their pasture during the day. They lived about half a mile out of town. During the summer, us children would walk the cow to pasture for the day and then we would walk out to get her before supper. I remember Mom also had some chickens in the barn. It must have saved a lot of money to have milk, cream and eggs to feed our large family.

When relatives came to visit for night, Mom would turn the kitchen table over and put the little ones inside the frame of the table. Helen and I and our cousins slept on the floor. No sleeping bags, no air mattresses or foam mattresses. We survived. We laughed and talked into the wee hours of the morning.

Mom had been very sick for a couple of years before she passed away. I could read one of her letters to Grandpa and Grandma. She told them her heart was very weak and her kidneys were shutting down. My doctor said it sounded like she had Rheumatic Fever. Many times when we got home from school, there was a note saying that Mom had been taken to the hospital in Saskatoon.

Mom was very happy when Lydia had Harvey, born on December 25, 1948.

back row: Bill, Lydia and Harvey, Dave and me;
front row; Helen, Dad and Mom

She was so happy to be a grandmother. I am glad she had the chance to know how wonderful being a Grandmother was, as I am sure she knew she didn't have much time left.

Our dear mother passed away December 17, 1949 of a brain aneurysm at the age of forty-seven years. At the time of her passing Lydia was twenty-three, married and had a little boy, Harvey, who was not quite a year old. Bill was nineteen years old; Corney, seventeen years; John, fourteen years; myself, twelve years and Helen, nine years old.

CHAPTER 4
And Then There Were Six

My five siblings were; the oldest, Lydia; next to her Bill (or Willie as we called him); Corney; John; I was the second youngest, and then my little sister Helen.

Lydia was born May 8, 1926. She was not happy as a teenager because she felt that it was unfair that she had to help as much around the house as she did. Very usual for any teenager to feel that way.

Lydia

She married too young. Mom and Dad did not approve of her choice of a new husband. They were against the marriage but her mind was made up. She spent many years regretting her decision. The things she never regretted were her six beautiful children. Harvey; Laura; Linda; Brita; Ernie and Melvin. Helen and I loved her dearly and wished she would stay with us after Mom passed away. But her husband wanted to stay near his mother. The many times Lydia came to visit were the best times for Helen and I. We just loved having her near and playing with her little ones. Lydia passed away on September 12, 1986 at the age of sixty years. Her last days were spent in the hospital at Nipawin after a long, painful battle with stomach cancer. I really have missed her as she was like a mother to Helen and me and when she died, we felt like we lost our mother all over again.

The three sisters; myself, Helen and Lydia

July 27, 1930 was the day William Alexander (Bill) was born. He was a very bright student in school. He studied very hard and got very good marks. He also was very musical and could play almost any instrument. In high school he had a very close friend Ken Wilkinson. Those two were always coming up with some new ideas and inventions. Ken lived a few miles out of town and they concocted a phone line between the two places using tin cans and wire strung along the fences. It worked too!! Bill went to Normal School in Saskatoon. That is what they called the school where people trained to be a teacher When he came home in the summer, he was always so good to Helen and I. He would pretend he was sleeping and make all kinds of sounds. Helen and I laughed and laughed. We had so much fun with him.

Bill, Helen and me

He then taught at Armley and Ridgedale, Saskatchewan. There he met the love of his life, Mildred Schilltroth who lived on a farm near Armley. They made a very good couple. They had a lovely family of four children; Lillian, Russell, Dianne and Sheila. Bill became a Conservation Officer with the Department of Natural Resources and later on became the Deputy Minister of Natural Resources for the Saskatchewan Government.

Bill as Conservation Officer for the DNR

Bill was gifted with the ability to talk to anyone he met and his sense of humour was enjoyed, not only by his family, but by all he met. With all these talents, he had many engagements as speakers at banquets etc. Sadly to say, he had numerous health problems and passed away December 2, 2000 with an aortic aneurism at the age of seventy years.

Cornelius Peter (Corney) was named after Grandpa Matthies. He was born on May 16, 1932. Corney was very brilliant in school. As Bill had to study hard to get very good marks, Corney got very good marks without studying. It took a while to realize that he had been blessed with a photographic memory. He would look at something once and would remember it. Being that Corney was so clever in school the teachers let him skip a grade. I don't remember what grade he skipped but when he was seventeen (birthday in May) he graduated from High School.

Corney, myself and Helen with a neighbour's daughter

He then went to Normal School for the required one year. So at just barely eighteen years, he was sent to a rural school near Nipawin to teach classes that could be from Grade One to Grade Ten. In the meantime, while he was training, Mom passed away. He had a very rough time of it until he met his future bride at a dance in Nipawin. It was love at first sight for both of them. He married Gladys Broten and left the teaching profession to become one of Calgarys' best. Corney spent many years as a Police Officer in Calgary. During this time, with the use his photographic memory, he received many citations from The City of Calgary Police Force.

Corney as an officer with the Calgary Police Force

After retiring he worked as a Security Guard at a Calgary Bank. Gladys and he had three beautiful children; Bruce, Ken and Sharon. Corney passed away very suddenly of a massive heart attack on April 23, 1983 at the age of fifty years. He was my best brother. I have really missed him.

John Robert was born June 6, 1935. He married Jean Kostiuk of Carrot River. They had two girls, Roxanne and Anita. He spent his life as a salesman for many, many companies. He passed away on July 27, 2012 of bladder cancer at the age of seventy-seven years.

I was born August 30, 1937. My parents only gave me one name, after my mother Annie. Everyone else in the family had two names except Lydia and me. Maybe they couldn't think of any girls names other than the one we got. Oh well, if that is the worst thing I have had to put up with in my life, I would indeed have been lucky. Being named after my mother grew more precious to me as I got older. After we married, Dad (Grandpa) preferred to call me Ann and I certainly liked that better than being called Annie.

Helen Amalia (there's that second name again), was born September 3, 1940. She was given her second name after Grandma Matthies. Helen was always a beautiful little girl. I was the plain one. I loved her dearly and after Mom passed away, I did all I could to keep her safe and happy.

Helen

It was as difficult at 12 years old for me to try to replace her mother, as it was difficult for Helen to accept me as such. We did fight but let someone else try to hurt us, we were quick to protect the other. Helen married Frank Remarchuk on November 7, 1959. They were the proud parents of five children; Debbie, Wendy, Cheryl, Heather and Michael. Frank worked for the Department of Indian Affairs, Therefore they spent many years living on Indian Reservations in North Central Saskatchewan where he taught the aboriginals. After some years they moved to Duck Lake where he taught at the Mission School. When

Frank retired, they moved to Saskatoon to be closer to their children. Helen passed away of colon cancer on December 29, 2001 at the age of 61 years. My heart was broken after losing my little sister who so often I felt was my own child. She is at peace now.

The Klassen Family; back row, l to r; Dad carrying Helen, Lydia, Mom; middle row; Bill, Corney, John and myself in the front row)

CHAPTER 5
Home Sweet Home

The village on the prairies was Aberdeen, Saskatchewan. It was a small farming community that depended on the district farmers for it's survival. The farmers in this area came from many ethnic backgrounds - they were Ukrainians, Germans, Scottish and British to name a few. It is now a bedroom community for commuters who work in Saskatoon.

I remember the town as not too small but also not large. There was a large sports ground with a large wooden grandstand. The concession was at the back and under the stands. There were a lot of ball games every summer. I kept the score at most of them. I think there were two reasons why I was given the honour of that position. Number one was that my two oldest brothers played ball and number two was that no one else would do it. It was better than what the umpires had to go through.

The sports ground was near the school and some of us would go to the concession booth under the grandstand at recess, where some of the more adventurous girls would have a cigarette. This was also where our school principal, Eugene Hamm, surprised us one day. We had to stay after school, when he lined us all up and asked each one "Were you smoking?" and each answered yes, until he got to me. I said no. So he started all over and asked each one, "Was Annie smoking?" to which each answered no. He told me he was very proud of me. And then proceeded to tell us how terrible smoking was and he wished he had never started. But even after that he didn't worry about setting a good example as he still continued to sneak down to the furnace room during classes to have a smoke.

The Empress Hotel was a three-story building which had a cafe and a bar. Helen and I and our friends spent a lot of time at the cafe. Helen also spent a good deal of time in the hotel lobby playing cribbage with the old retired bachelors that called the hotel their home. I never did or have yet to this day, learned to play cribbage.

Nick's Barber Shop and Pool Hall was one of the activity centres for the men in town. Not only for playing pool but also to get together to talk about the weather and solve all the problems that the government of the day couldn't solve. Dad did spend some time at the Pool Hall but I think it was more to visit than to play pool. It was strictly forbidden for females to enter the Pool Hall. If we went in, we could not go past the Barber Shop at the front. Unknown to Dad, there were a few rare occasions when after his closing hours at night, Nick would let some of us girls in the back door to try to shoot pool. He taught us to be very careful so we wouldn't rip the cloth. Dad always got his hair cut there. His three boys and Helen and I were never privileged enough to have Nick cut our hair. Dad did so, porridge bowl and all. He did cut Helen and my hair in steps. Bangs were the first step, then in front of the ears, the second and lastly the third at the base of the neck. He said it was the style but we thought it strange that none of our friends ever had the same haircut. Oh well, with so many children he saved a lot of money by being the family hairdresser

Butch's Meat Market was another important place in town. His meat was top quality and he had a good variety of meat. The most important part of the Meat Market was the table in the back room where Butch and his friends, Dad included, spent hours playing "schmeer." Us kids were never allowed to go back there. I'm sure they never played for money as I don't think Dad would ever have had enough money to play at that time. But... maybe he was a very good player and supplemented our income from that. If so, we certainly never heard about it.

The CNR Train Station was a place that Helen and I spent a lot of time at. The station agent didn't mind us being there. We loved seeing the trains come in and the conductors got to know us by our first names. There was nothing we loved more than meeting the train when Lydia and her children came to visit from Gronlid.

The Aberdeen Telephone Office was operated by a very lovely lady who would teach us how to connect calls after she answered them. At that time, I felt my destiny was to become a telephone operator. But that never came to pass.

The Canadian Bank of Commerce had been a large old brick building which in the 50's was replaced by a new building erected on Main Street just at the corner from our place.

The Canadian Bank of Commerce where I worked.
My friend Bernice Miner on steps

This was the only banking institution in Aberdeen. I worked in this bank for two years before I got married. Helen also worked there before she was married. This building still exists in Aberdeen and was used as a cafe. The Canadian Bank of Commerce has closed and they have built a new building on Main Street that now houses Affinity Credit Union.

Aberdeen Community Hall was the centre of almost all community events. The school had their Christmas Concerts there each December. I will never forget the year when I was in high school and we put on the play "The Christmas Carol" at the Christmas Concert. I was in it but don't remember what part I played. I'm sure it wasn't a very important part. Each year, after the Concert was over we all were given a bag of treats (which consisted of hard candies and an orange). I didn't like hard candy then and I still don't like them now. Then, when it was all over, came the best of all. We ran home because we knew Lydia and the children had arrived on the train. The old Community Hall was in need of major repairs so was dismantled sometime after 1977 and a large new Community Hall was built on the former sports ground.

The Canadian Legion Hall was a fairly new building at that time. The only time that we could go inside was on Remembrance Day. The Remembrance Day Service was held at the Community Hall. In the days we belonged to the CGIT, after the Service was over, we would walk as a group with the Legion to the Legion Hall where we were served lunch and hot chocolate. The adults had coffee and stronger? drinks. Some years the walk was VERY COLD. I recall the walk being called off at least one year because of the weather. Dad faithfully went to the Remembrance day Service although he was never in the Legion. Mennonites never served in the war as they were considered "conscientious objectors." This meant that their religion objected to violence. I think Dad felt better to go and show honour and respect to the ones that did. When Dad was the Mayor for five years, he always placed a wreath for the Town. At that time, the Bank Manager was Mr James Riches. He and his wife had two sons, Bill and Bob. Both boys joined the army. Bill was killed in the war and earned a Mention in Dispatches for bravery. Bob returned home safely and was presented with a Distinguished Flying Cross for bravery under fire. I have never attended a Remembrance Day Service without remembering Mr and Mrs Riches presenting a wreath to honour their two sons. It was very emotional and now as a mother and grandmother, I really know just how much of a sacrifice they made to keep our country free.

With all the problems with the health system these days, Aberdeen was lucky in those days to have their own doctor and druggist - Dr James Holmes. He practised in Aberdeen for over 40 years. He brought all of us Klassen children into the world in our own house. Doctor Holmes was very gentle. During my "Calamity Annie" stage, I visited him more than once.

CHAPTER 6
Children at Play

One summer Dad decided all of us would go to Rabbit Lake to visit Grandpa and Grandma Matthies. He borrowed a truck from a farmer. It had a wooden box on the back. Of course in those days it wasn't a very fancy truck. Dad, Mom and Helen got in the front and the boys and myself got in the back. Without saying, a truck in those days didn't travel very fast and there were no laws yet about riding in the back of a truck, so we weren't in any danger. The closer we got to Rabbit Lake, we could tell it had rained as the road was slippery. In those days, there was no pavement on the roads. Then there were hills we had to climb. More than once the boys had to get out and push the truck up the hills. We finally managed to get there. What a great time we had! I still remember the good earth smell from an old tumbled down pig barn at the farm. I am not joking when I say that. It had been many, many years since they had pigs and the manure had returned to good rich soil. We played with our cousins and had a lot of fun at Grandpa and Grandma's farm. I also remember the beautiful flowers that Grandma grew. We loved Grandpa and Grandma very much and Mom was very happy to be with them again.

Back row l to r; Uncle Abe, Mom, Grandpa, Grandma, Uncle John and
Aunt Mary Huebert; front row l to r; Helen, myself, Alfred Huebert

The Canadian Legion Hall was across the street from the
"bump." The "bump" was where the sidewalk ended and as
it was above level with the road, there was a drop at the
end of the sidewalk. Helen and I would ride bike down
the sidewalk on Main Street until we got to the "bump."
We thought the drop was very far down but after we grew
up we realized it wasn't very deep at all.

I always loved dolls. Even as a mother and grandmother, I
still love dolls. You may not believe this, but I DO NOT
play with them anymore!

Myself and one of my dolls

I was probably about eight years old when we got the Eaton's Christmas Catalogue. Inside, I found the doll of my dreams! Barbara Ann Scott was a famous figure skater in the 40's and there was a doll of Barbara Ann Scott. She had a royal blue velvet figure skating dress with a white feather trim on the bottom. AND she was wearing skates! I really, really, wanted her. I asked Mom if I could get that doll. I don't remember what it cost. Mom said if I earned some of the money, she would give me the rest. I was willing to do anything. I helped Dad, I helped Mom and it just didn't look like I was going to be able to get it. Then one day as I was walking down the street, I saw an envelope lying on the street beside the sidewalk. I picked it up and looked inside. There was a lot of money inside. I ran home and showed Mom, all excited because I finally had enough money to buy the Barbara Ann Scott doll. Mom counted the money. Sixty dollars! (that was a lot in those days). She saw a name on the front of the envelope. "Annie,"she said, "You can't keep this money." It belonged to an old man in town. It was his pension money. I knew I had to give it back to him. Mom and I went to visit him and gave him the envelope. He was so happy. He said he lost it and it was all the money he had to live on for the month. I was so sad, but knew it was what I had to do. Shortly after that, I met him on the street. He gave me a sealed envelope and told me not to open it until I got home. I ran home as fast as I could. Mom opened the envelope. Inside was a thank you note for me AND A FIVE DOLLAR BILL! Mom said that she would give me the rest so I could order the doll. I treasured my Barbara Ann Scott doll for years until one day after Mom had passed away, I couldn't find her. I looked everywhere. She was not to be found. As we didn't lock our doors in those days, someone may have come in and taken her. Last summer I finally had my chance to see another Barbara Ann Scott doll at a doll show in Moose Jaw. This one was wearing a red skating outfit. Just as beautiful as my Barbara Ann Scott doll was many years ago.

Dad built a playhouse for Helen and I when we were growing up. Little did we know then that keeping house would be put into reality much sooner than we ever imagined.

Helen sitting in front of the playhouse that Dad built for us

I'm not sure whether it was the summer of 1947 or 1948, Helen and I travelled by train to visit Lydia and Dave. We took the train to Melfort and from there another train to Gronlid. Lydia and Dave picked us up and drove us to their home. That summer they were looking after a farm for a neighbour who lived on the "flat." The "flat" was the land next to the North Saskatchewan River. It was very level. We descended a densely tree covered hillside to get there. It was just beautiful on the "flat." Helen and I loved to play outside. There was so much to see. One afternoon Lydia and Dave drove into Gronlid and left us alone. We played all day and later on we decided we would walk down the road that led to the road going up the hillside. We didn't walk too far when we decided to go back. We knew they must be coming because we heard someone sneezing a few times. Later, when Lydia and Dave got back, we told them about someone sneezing. They both quickly looked at each other and I caught the worried expressions on their faces. When asked if we did something wrong, they finally told us that would have been bears we heard. We were warned never to leave the yard again at any time. We never argued.

I also vaguely remember going to visit Lydia and Dave with Mom and Dad and sleeping in the old house that Dave's parents lived in. A thunderstorm came up in the night. Dave's mother woke us all up and we all had to sit in the living room together, with the kerosine lamps lit, until the storm was over. A couple of deductions were made by us; if lightening struck, she wanted us all to die at once; or she maybe she thought the light would scare the lightning away. Who knows, but we did survive.

There was a sidewalk from the Blacksmith Shop to Main Street. The town put this unusual sidewalk in. It was made up of cinders (hard, sharp ashes from the trains.) So every summer we had a contest to see who could be the first one to walk the full length of this sidewalk in bare feet. No wonder I have so much trouble with my feet now.

CHAPTER 7
The Day the
Colour Went Out Of The World

Mom had been quite ill for a couple of years before she passed away. I remember one Sunday morning we had planned to go to Langham after church, to visit some friends. I was sitting in the living room as Mom came into it from the bedroom. I asked her if we were going to see our friends today. Mom suddenly collapsed and passed out. I called Dad, who was in the kitchen. It seemed like hours before he got there but I'm sure it was seconds. Sometimes as parents, especially when we are upset, we say things to our children without dreaming the impact those words can make on our children. If I ever did so to our children I sincerely apologize.

Dad came in, put Mom's head in his lap and said, "This is what happens when you kids fight so much." I don't remember too clearly what happened that day, other than the ambulance came after some time and took Mom to the hospital in Saskatoon. Helen and I hugged each other and swore we would never fight again.

Mom came home after a few days but this repeated itself, (I can't remember how many times.) Each time, when Helen and I came home from school and found a note saying Mom had gone to the hospital, Helen and I would get down on our knees and pray that God would please bring Mom home. We promised we would never fight again. As we were still children, it seemed like we did fight again, no matter how hard we tried not to.

I was twelve years old. Early in the morning of December 17, 1949, I woke up to hear Mom crying in German what is translated to, "My head, my head." I closed my eyes and saw a tombstone. I knew then what was going to happen.

After a while the ambulance came to take her away. The neighbour lady had come over and she stood at the window with Helen and me as the ambulance pulled away. She said, "Say good bye to your Mom. She won't be back." I said a quiet "Good bye Mom." I knew then that Mom was not going to make it because we had been fighting again.

After that Helen and I went over to our friend Mary's to play until Dad got back. We had a good time playing and after a big supper, Mary, Helen and I went skating.

We had been skating for some time when one of our brothers came to tell us to come home. On the way home he was whistling. I thought to myself, "This is good. Mom must be okay or he wouldn't be whistling." About a block away from our house, he stopped whistling. I knew then this was not good. We walked into the house. Dad and our other brothers were sitting at the table crying. Dad came, put his arms around Helen and I and told us that Mom didn't make it. I knew it. We had been fighting. This ran through my mind over and over. I couldn't cry but everyone else was. So I pretended to cry. I went to the bathroom and thought that they would think I was terrible for not crying so I sobbed loudly.

When it was bedtime, Dad told Helen and me we could sleep with him. Helen crawled into the middle and I at the back. I couldn't go to sleep for a long time. Sometime later there was a knock on the door. It was Mary's dad. He said "Well, Bill." "It's over," Dad answered.

The next few days were a blur to me. I knew Lydia and Dave came. There were other people that came and went, but my mind was a blank. I do remember Lydia and I washing the floor. Suddenly I didn't feel good and told Lydia so. She said, "You are just trying to get out of work." She no sooner said it when I passed out.

I don't know how long I was out but I woke up in bed. The doctor came and I couldn't understand why but I didn't feel good. I still hadn't cried.

The funeral was set for December 23.

The winter of 1949 was a very bad winter with a lot of snow and many storms. Most roads were blocked and the highway to Saskatoon was no exception. So Mom's casket was shipped out to Aberdeen by train on December 22 and was placed in the basement of the church.

Dad, Lydia and the boys went to the church to see Mom. I was still in bed and Helen wanted to stay with me. After all she was only nine years old. When they got back, I asked my brother how she looked. He said she had a smile on her face. Then the flood gates opened and for the first time since I had woken up the morning Mom passed away. I cried and cried and cried. I never thought this before but as I am writing now, I am thinking that maybe I thought Mom would be mad at us for fighting and causing her to die. But if she had a smile on her face she mustn't be mad at us. How a child's mind works sometimes.

The day of the funeral, I was still in bed. Helen cried and told me she didn't want to go to the funeral. She asked if I would ask Dad if she could stay with me. Of course I did and Dad let her stay.

The neighbour lady Mrs McKechnie came over to stay with Helen and me during the funeral. She brought me a bowl of borscht to eat. I tasted it but I couldn't understand why it was so flat. Helen thought it was great.

The next day was Christmas Eve. I woke up in the morning feeling very good. I stepped out of bed and immediately collapsed. So I guess I didn't get better that quickly.

Two days after the service was Christmas Day. A happy time for others but not in our household. I couldn't understand how people could be so happy when we were so sad in our house. Later that morning, there was a knock on the door. It was Mr Kruger, a friend of Dad's. He brought a crockinole board as a present for all of us. What a wonderful, kind thing for him to do! That day was spent by all of us playing crockinole for hours on end. We all had sore fingers but how nice to be able to forget our sadness even for a minute.

Life went on, but for Dad, Helen and me, it was very lonely. Dad had begged Lydia and Dave to come home, live with us for free and he would supply them with free food, if only they would look after Helen and me. But Dave insisted that he needed to be close to his mother. Dad did try, but many a morning Helen and I woke up to the smell of burnt toast. Or Dad waking us up and telling us to get up because he thought the oil space heater was going to blow up. I guess Mom was the one that looked after that, too.

The times I missed Mom the most was coming home to an empty and quiet house and no baking smells. Everything seemed so colourless for years. It wasn't until I met your Dad (Grandpa) that true colour was once again restored to my world.

CHAPTER 8
Helping Hands

Things in our household were really scary for the first while after mom passed away. I was only twelve, Helen was only nine and John never helped much at any time. I didn't know or care to keep the house clean. Dad had never lifted a finger in the house before Mom passed away. He never made a meal and now he was left with three children to look after and feed. Mom, sick as she was, did it all. Although later on Dad learned to make the best borscht that I have ever eaten.

I think it was the next summer that Dad decided he needed help. One Sunday Dad, Helen and I got into the car and drove to a farm about 10 miles away. This family had many children and we ending up taking one of the daughters home with us. I would say she was in her late teens. In the short time she stayed with us as a housekeeper, never again did we ever call her by her name. We nicknamed her "Snake Eyes." We did not like her. She was bossy, yelled at us, and tried to make us do all her work. Dad caught on fast and ....away she went.

Then after some months a woman named Betty Schellenberg, who lived in town, began to come to our house in the daytime. She would have been in her 30's and had been born with very weak legs. So she was quite bow legged. We loved her!! She was wonderful to us. She cleaned the house, baked bread, made meals and she loved us. We wished Dad would marry her, but she was not in good health. So by the time she had to quit working, she had taught me how to keep Helen and my hair neat and how to keep the house clean.

Helen and myself

We really missed her when she had to go and visited her often as her family lived in town. She died not many years after that.

A couple of our girlfriends, who were sisters, lived in town. Then house cleaning got to be a fun game. One Saturday, they would come to our house and the four of us would clean our house, top to bottom. Wash floors and dust, change beds and wash clothes. The next week we would go to their house and do the same. Their mother had no objection. Until one day their mother told them they couldn't come to our house anymore, as there was no mother around, but we could come to their house. All four of us cried together. To think that losing our mother wasn't enough punishment for two young girls, and then to think our house wasn't safe for her girls. We did go there once in a while but not very often. And they came to our house sometimes too, unknown to their mother. After that, the game began to be work. I was left with doing it myself. But by that time, I really didn't mind it. It was good to have a clean house.

The ironic thing was one day the youngest sister and her mother went for a holiday. They were gone for about six months. When they came home we were so happy to see our friend we rushed over to see her. She had gained a lot of weight and was very quiet. It didn't take too long to figure out what had happened. And she wasn't safe in our house?

A couple of years later, on a weekend, a lady and her son (about my age), came to visit for the weekend. They stayed at the hotel. She was from Waldheim, if I remember correctly. Dad told us they were coming to visit. He said that they might get married. Helen and I were so excited! We were going to have a mother again! But.... after the weekend, she never came back. Dad didn't even talk about it. And we didn't dare ask! Years later, after your Dad (Grandpa) and I were married, my Dad came to visit. By then I was brave enough to ask him what had happened. Why didn't she come back? I told him we were so excited about having a mother again. Dad told me, "Remember the son she had?" I said yes. He said that weekend was enough for him to see that her son would be placed ahead of us two girls in everything, and he couldn't do that to us. I gave him a big hug and thanked him. I knew what a lonely man he was, and to think he would give up what could have been a happier life for himself so that we could be happier.

CHAPTER 9
The Faith that Keeps Us Going

Our family went to church every Sunday and sometimes twice on a Sunday.

Aberdeen Mennonite Conference Church that we attended

Mom would sit at the back of the congregation so her little ones would not disturb anyone else. Mom had a beautiful voice. I guess I inherited that from her, though I have never considered myself to have the voice she had.

On Sunday morning, we always went to Sunday School while mom and dad went to church. After church we would have company come in for dinner and to spend the day, or we would go visit at friends that lived on a farm. What fun!!

Helen and I loved going to Sunday School and also Daily Vacation Bible School in the summer. There were so many good choruses we learned to sing. Such as "This Little Light of Mine," and "Climb, Climb Up Sunshine Mountain."

When we were little children, someone told us that during services, there was a man standing at the back of the church, with a long pole and any children that didn't behave, he would touch their heads with the pole so everyone knew who was misbehaving. We weren't too sure if it was right or not and none of us dared misbehave too much to find out. Quite often in the afternoons we had, what was called (translation from German) Young Peoples Program. At this program they had musical numbers and then anyone else who wished, could come forward and perform.

These programs were so enjoyable. I felt the best musical numbers were when the Men's quartet sang such songs as, "Hear Dem Bells" and "On the Jericho Road," as well as other beautiful numbers. Those quartets could rival any of the best Men's Gospel Quartets I have ever heard.

Even before Mom passed away, I went to a Sunday School Retreat at the Mennonite Youth farm at Rosthern. I think I must have been about 10 years old. Most of my friends went too. The Youth Farm had two very large hip roofed barns. One for horses and one for the milk cows. Children from all over Saskatchewan came to this Retreat. The girls slept on blankets in the hay loft of the horse barn along with the women leaders. The boys slept in the hay loft of the milk cow barn, also with the men who were leaders. There was nothing as much fun as sleeping up there with my friends. If there were mice, we never noticed.

I do remember this good-looking reddish haired boy, probably around 15 years old, that came over and rode one of the horses in the corral at the horse barn. I thought he was the dreamiest looking guy I had ever seen. I would have given anything if he had noticed me, but I don't think he even saw me. He was showing off and trying to impress the older girls. Years after we were married and looking at pictures of your Dad (Grandpa) when he was younger and finding out he had been at the retreat the same year as I had, I realized that good-looking reddish haired boy was Dad (Grandpa). If you're meant to be together, you will be together.

The leaders at the Retreat were high pressure salesmen for God. Not that God wants anyone to be high pressured into knowing Him. Listening to them made me feel that I really wanted to know Him better. So I asked God to come into my heart. I have never had such a really good feeling. I knew it couldn't be a wrong decision or I wouldn't feel so good. This belief that I could go through anything with God at my side, has helped keep me strong through many difficult times in my life. It's this faith that makes me believe that someday I could meet my family again.

I began singing alto in the Mennonite Choir at probably fourteen years old. The choir consisted of about two dozen people with all four parts being sung - soprano, alto, tenor and bass. Even now, there are not many churches, if any, that can sing as good as the people in the Mennonite

Churches. A God given gift to me was that I could sing alto, just as my mother did. I could sing by ear and also, as I had taught myself to read music, I was able to read the music that the choir had and sing along with them. The very capable leader of the choir was Ike Thiessen. We all enjoyed him and I loved the other members of the choir. I was the youngest. We also sang German songs. I really didn't know how to read German, but with help, I stumbled through it. I really enjoyed singing in this choir. One memory that stands out in my mind was the time we practised before Mothers Day. The song he had chosen was "Memories of Mother." I started singing but as the words of the song sank in, I no longer could see through my tears and I ran out and home. I noticed that Ike stopped at the Blacksmith Shop after practise. Another time that missing Mom was almost unbearable.

The Mennonite Church was very strict in many ways. We were not allowed to dance. The children of the so-called "important families" in the church, would have parties and dance and never invite us. To us it was "do as I say, not as I do." I kept going to church as I had enough other friends and I didn't feel like I needed them either. Helen was more rebellious than myself and joined the United Church. Dad was very upset. I told him she was better off in that church because she would then go to church more often. She did. When I met your Dad (Grandpa), who was also a Mennonite, I was glad I had decided to stay in the church.

As I have said, Mennonites were not allowed to go to dances. All our friends went. So after I graduated from school and started working in the bank, the first dance that came up, I went to Dad and told him I was going to the dance. He said "No. You're not!" to which I defiantly replied, "Yes I am. You taught me to have a mind of my own, and now I'm using it!" I told him whom I was going with and when I would be home and he never said anymore. The next dance that came up, Helen, who was three years my junior, asked Dad if she could go. He told her she could, as long as I went. That proved what I had always suspected. HE DID LOVE HELEN MORE THAN ME!!

CHAPTER 10
Readin' 'Ritin' and 'Rithmetic

Aberdeen School was an old red brick school house on the north end of town.

Aberdeen School

It housed grades one to twelve. There was a very wide hallway with wide stairs at each end that led to the basement. At the end of the hall was the dreaded Principal's

Office. The only time we got to see the inside, was when we were in trouble. Some boys got to see it very often.

We had to walk about five blocks to school each day, wind, rain, snow or sun. If we took the short cut, behind the rink and in front of the water dugout, we could cut that down about half a block. There were varied times that it took us to walk to school, depending on the weather, or if we did or didn't do our homework, or numerous other reasons. A new, state of the art school and gymnasium was built in the 60's next to the old school.

Punishment in those days was to hold out your hand and receive slaps from the belt kept in the office and always administered by Mr Hamm, the school's principal. This only happened when there were serious demeanours. I don't ever recall any of us getting it except for one of my brothers. One of Dad's rules was, if you got a strapping in school you got one at home. Years later, Dad asked me if I remembered when my brother got the strap. I said yes. He told me that when he went to give him his just punishment, my brother kept yelling "Seven, I only got seven." Dad said he was only going to give him a couple but my brother insisted on seven - so he gave him seven. Nowadays this would be called abuse but those lickings certainly helped to get the point across.

At the bottom of the back stairs was a chemistry lab. At one time, some of the boys were experimenting and blew a hole in the cement floor. I didn't know for sure but I had a sneaking suspicion that the Klassen boys were involved in that experiment.

School was really a lot of fun. There was a big playground outside with two sets of swings, big ones and small ones and also teeter totters. In the winter we curled with frozen jam cans on the ice that the boys made behind the school.

Every morning before school, we sang "O Canada," recited the "Lord's Prayer," and sang "God Save the King," at assembly in the hall before classes began. Every classroom had a picture hanging on the front wall, of King George VI, (until 1952) and then Queen Elizabeth II after that. Their pictures were also hanging in every other community place (except church). Everyone was very patriotic in those days. After we were married, Grandma Brown showed me a scrapbook of pictures that she had collected of the Royal Family.

Eugene Hamm was the principal most of the years that I went to school. He made subjects like Art History and Algebra, fun to learn. I had many teachers, some good and some bad but he was the best. Just like the students, some good and some bad. My favourite subjects were Art, Literature, Writing and Arithmetic. I was always a very average student. When I was in Grade Twelve, I had enough credits to pass. I figured Home Ec was so-o-o easy, because after all I had been looking after the house for some years. I never took the subject but elected to write the exam. I received 21% in my exam. So much for thinking I knew all there was to looking after a house.

During an Art History class, as Mr Hamm was showing us some nude statues that were in ancient Rome, a girl standing behind him pretended to trace a flea walking across the bald area on Mr Hamm's head. I began to laugh. Thinking I was laughing at the nude statues, Mr Hamm turned around angrily, asking me what I was laughing at. I meekly answered, "Nothing." He replied, "It sure doesn't take much to make you laugh, does it?" I certainly wasn't going to get that other girl in trouble.

Every May, all the schools in the district would come to town to have a Track and Field Meet at the Sports grounds. The rural schools had interesting names such as Strawberry Valley, Corn Valley, Lily South, Lily North, Hesseldale, Friedland, Old Trail, River Park, Pretoria, and New Steinbach. The winners from our Meet then went on to Elstow for the Unit Meet. I went to Elstow every year. Elstow was a small town to the south of Aberdeen. I was very athletic when I was young as I was very thin. Probably from eating Dads' fried side pork and fried potatoes almost every day. (I think Dr Atkins should be questioned about where he got his well known diet from.) My favourite sports at Field Meets were high jump, broad jump, and racing in that order. Each year I would sprain my ankle while high jumping and Dad would take me to see Mrs Peters. She lived on a farm in the country with her family. She was, what the close translation from German would be called a "bone fixer." She never ever took any training for this but for some unexplained reason, she could always fix things like sprains. After fixing my ankle and then bandaging it, she told me not to jump anymore that season. In a day or two I was at it again. I won a lot of ribbons in especially high jumping, mostly red.

Myself broad jumping at the School Field Meet

Before the Track and Field Meet started, everyone lined up on the Sports ground with their own schools and we all sang "God Save the King." At that time we had a king, King George VI, the present Queen Elizabeth's father.

All of the schools had a ball team so after the other activities were over, we would have a ball tournament. I never was too good at ball but we had enough other ones to play, so I kept the score. When everything was over, we all lined up and each of us were given a five cent coupon to go to the hotel for a free ice cream cone. They were big, very hard ice cream cones. We didn't know what soft ice cream was in those days. The only soft ice cream we knew of was when we didn't eat it fast enough on a hot day.

The Grade Twelve Class I was in, never had a graduation. We were asked to go to a tea by the local IODE (Imperial Daughters of the Empire). I was asked to give a speech thanking them. That was as close to valedictorian that I ever got. The next year, the Grade Twelve Class had a Graduation. We felt cheated. When Helen graduated from Grade Twelve, she wore my wedding dress. She looked beautiful!

The red brick school was used as a Senior Centre until in the 90's when they had it taken down to allow more playground space.

CHAPTER 11
"Calamity Annie"

As Dad was a blacksmith, he had various tools to help him with his work. By tools, I don't only mean hammers, screw drivers etc. He had large tools. A forge, in which he had a coal fire that he heated up with a set of bellows attached to the forge. In this he would heat the ploughshares, etc. so that they would be red hot. He would take his sledge hammer (very big and heavy) and he would put the red hot ploughshare on an anvil (a large heavy iron with a flat top on it and a pointed end on it.) Then he would pound it until it had a sharp edge. That alone should tell you how powerful a man he was. He had other equipment that was powered by a medium sized gas engine. This engine had a large wheel on the outside. On this wheel was a hub (centre rod) sticking a fair ways out on the middle of it. There was a smaller wheel on the other side of the engine that had a belt attached to other equipment so they would work. When I was fairly small, us little ones liked to stand with our tummies on the hub as the machine was running. It would tickle us. One day I had on a loose dress and as I stood up to the hub, my dress wound up tighter and tighter on the hub, until it threw me and the motor stopped.

Mom told me later, that it knocked me out and Dad had to use a knife to cut me off the hub. Dad rushed me to Dr Holmes. I don't know what all happened to me but I have a scar at the bottom of my front teeth that probably was from that accident. They never really said, but I think I really scared them. After that, Dad cut the hub even with the wheel so that wouldn't happen again.

The summer after mom passed away (which would make me twelve years old) my brothers Bill and Corney built a merry-go-round. They were home for the summer, as they were both teachers and had the summers off. This merry-go-round consisted of a beam attached to the pole in the centre with a large bolt. They hung a wash tub on each end of the beam. To ride, someone would push the wash tub end to make it go in a circle. One day Bill and Corney went to Saskatoon and left strict orders NOT TO USE THE MERRY-GO-ROUND! But the temptation was too great, so I climbed in one tub and a friend climbed in the other tub. My brother John pushed us. All was fine until we went flying. When I came to, I remember my head hurting. I ran to the house. That day's Saskatoon Star Phoenix had just been delivered, so I picked it up and started rubbing my head. I looked at the paper and it was full of blood. All I could think of was, "Is Dad ever going to be mad. He hasn't read this yet." I guess the others called dad over. The large bolt had hit me on the top of my head. Dad immediately took me to Doctor Holmes. He shaved the top of my head and put in some stitches. I'm not sure how many but I still have the scar to prove it. When the boys came home from Saskatoon, we found out why the sudden flight. They had loosened the bolt in the middle. After all, we were forbidden to use it. I think they felt pretty bad about it as they took it down the next day. Or maybe it was because of a strong suggestion made by Dad.

I remember that I just loved hanging around in the shop. The smell was so good. Sukanen Museum south of Moose Jaw has a blacksmith shop. I love that smell in there as it is the same as it was in Dad's shop. As I mentioned, Dad would heat metal red hot before he worked on it. I have a scar on the palm of my right hand and one on the front of the top of my left leg that would be from getting too close to hot metal in the shop.

Imagine the surprise and shock I got when Helen and me came home from Lydia's one summer. I ran out of the house and ran to the back alley to go see our friends. Suddenly I was lying face first in the dirt. Kids had been going through our yard so dad put a wire across the pathway. He was working in the shop and had forgot to tell us.

There is a family story that my brother hit me over the nose with a doll when I was little and in the crib. When I went for my pituitary surgery, they told me they couldn't go through my nose for my surgery as it had been broken at one time. So enough said about that.

I finally grew out of my clumsy stage only to have it revived when I got older. Oh well, you have to have something to talk about.

CHAPTER 12
Music Makes the World Go Round

Any community event that took place, always started with "God Save the King" (or Queen) and ended with "O Canada." Almost everything that went on in the Community Hall had a sing song. Eva Hamm, wife of the School Principal and daughter of our old neighbour, Mrs McKechnie, played fantastic music on the piano as everyone sang the good old songs, (even then they were old songs,) such as "Daisy, Daisy," "Neath the Shade of the Old Apple Tree," "The West the Nest and You," "It's Only A Shanty in Old Shanty Town," "Darktown Strutters Ball," "Five Foot Two," and others too numerous to mention. That is one thing that people our age still miss today - the good old sing songs where everyone joined in, sometimes with beautiful harmony. I decided that someday I was going to try to play almost as good as Eva.

I don't recall how old I was when Dad bought us an old pump organ. I don't know if he bought it or if someone gave him the organ for the work he had done for them. I was in heaven! I just loved it. I could play by ear but I did buy a Mammoth Music book from babysitting money I had earned. I did get one music lesson from my friend Mary. I paid her twenty-five cents for it. There also was a school teacher that taught some of us how to chord with our left hand. I didn't realize at that time what a God given gift it was to be able to play by ear.

I would sit down in the evening and start playing songs, by music and by ear. About midnight Dad would call out and tell me it was time to go to bed. I am so glad your Dad (Grandpa) enjoys listening to me play the piano. I now do quit playing long before midnight. I don't think Dad (Grandpa) would be as tolerant as my Dad was.

My family was very musical except for Lydia and Corney. Lydia knew she couldn't hold a tune, so didn't sing too much. But Corney didn't know, or didn't care that he couldn't hold a tune and he sang and sang. Leaving the house didn't help because he just sang louder. We were forced to leave the yard at the times when the music bug hit him.

Bill was a very good musician. He could play almost any instrument. He had an instrument handed down to him called a "sweet potato." This was a wind instrument that was shaped like a potato. I have no idea just where it came from or where it ended up. He also wrote many very good songs as well as some very humorous songs. He sang these with his very beautiful singing voice. Many times when he was home, we would have a great musical evening with Bill on the guitar and me on the organ. Dad really enjoyed those evenings. Those were great times!!

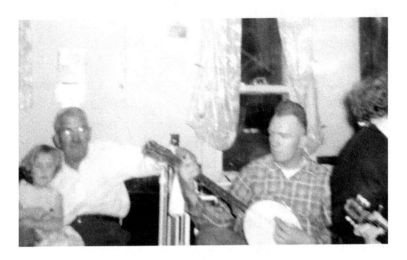

Brita (Lydia's daughter) and Dad with Bill on the banjo and myself on the organ, making music at home

We also travelled by train to spend some time with Bill when he taught at Armley. He lived in a small teacherage (resident for teacher). I think we maybe spent most or all of our time at the home of the parents of Bill's girlfriend, Mildred at the time, (and his wife later,) Mr and Mrs Schilltroth. What a great couple they were!! What a great time we had. No wonder Mildred was such a lovely person. Their farm had a small river running through it and there were so many beautiful trees. Bill also took us to visit this musical family. To us they seemed to be real hillbillies. They were very friendly and treated us great. Then the music began. They had several sons and each played a different musical instrument. Their mother played the piano. I have never seen a piano that has been more played than that one. The keys all had holes in them, worn out by so much playing. Bill also played with them. The music was fabulous! Real Bluegrass style!

Helen had a beautiful singing voice and her and I used to sing duets together. She never liked doing that but she did want me to teach her to play a song on the organ. The song she picked out was "Asleep in Jesus." This was a funeral song. I tried to convince her to learn to play something like "You Are My Sunshine," or "Beautiful, Beautiful Brown Eyes," but no, her mind was made up. So I taught her to play "Asleep in Jesus." I regretted that many times as I listened to her play it over and over again and again. She did play it well though, thank goodness. It could have been worse. She could have wanted to learn to play the fiddle!

Every Friday evening there was a dance in the Community Hall with live music. The bands were mostly local people. One of the bands that played was formed by a man that I worked with in the bank. I never really learned to dance as when we had dances in school, I was always playing the piano. But that music was really great!! And still is!! Now you know why Dad (Grandpa) and I enjoy listening to Saturday Dance Party on CKWW.

I am so glad that I lived in the years of the ACT Amateur Hour. The Amateur Hour, (which actually lasted for hours,) was a travelling radio show sponsored by the Associated Canadian Travellers. Each Saturday night this show was broadcast from various communities in Saskatchewan. They also came to Aberdeen. The talent from these shows was sometimes excellent and sometimes much to be desired. But everyone had a chance to perform and share their talent with others. When it came to Aberdeen the hall was full. We too shared our talent with everyone. Other Saturdays we stay tuned to the radio until the wee hours of the morning, listening to the show from other communities. I recently was told by a gentleman who was a member of the ACT in those days, when the Amateur Hour started to decline, they put on a dance following the show. This was met with much enthusiasm and the show immediately picked up and continued for many more years.

CHAPTER 13
A Little of This...A Little of That

The summer after Mom passed away, the Circus was coming to town. But of course we didn't get excited about it as we knew Dad couldn't afford to buy us tickets. The day of the Circus, I met a lady who lived in town. She gave me money and said, "Now you can go to the Circus, Annie." Knowing I wouldn't go and leave Helen at home and without thinking that I might sound ungrateful, I asked, "Do you have enough for Helen too?" She, it seemed, unwillingly, gave me enough for Helen too. Was I ungrateful or was she the one that was insensitive? I know we both enjoyed the Circus.

One day Helen and I went to the basement to snoop. The basement walls were boarded part way up and then rest was dirt. We knew there were mice down there and we made lots of noise to scare them off. There was quite a shelf of dirt that went under the house. We snooped here and there and finally our curiosity was rewarded. We found a fur neck piece. It had a fox head on it. It was dusty but in pretty good shape. We took turns wearing this and pretending we were ladies of luxury. Mom must have worn this when she was younger and probably felt the same way as we did with it on. We never did find out the real story of it and why it was on the dirt shelf in the basement. Maybe the mice knew but they would never tell.

I would be remiss if I didn't tell you about Aberdeen's water supply. As I mentioned before, there was a dugout behind the rink. We had running water, or sometimes walking water. Dad built a cart and put a small barrel on it. The cart had large iron wheels. It was VERY noisy. I'm sure everyone in town knew when the Klassens' got their water. If you think you have had embarrassing things happen to you as a child, I am positive it was not as embarrassing as when we had to get a barrel of water. For some reason, John was never around and the task fell to Helen and I. Until the day Helen went on strike and refused to pull that squeaking, squawking monstrosity those three agonizing blocks from the dugout to home. I was a sucker again and did it, so Dad wouldn't have to take time away from his work to do it. There were times that I don't think he was that busy, but I don't think he could stand the embarrassment either.

Helen and I didn't always make Dad's job easier. I did more housework than Helen but then I was older. One evening after supper, it was Helen's turn to do dishes. She refused and ordinarily I would have done them, but this time I was determined to make her do them. So after the waiting game, she finally got up, gathered all the dishes (from the three of us), in one armful and began to walk across the dining room to the kitchen. Suddenly she stumbled, dropped the dishes and broke every single dish. Dad was furious at her. She won again! She only had to wash the cutlery. Then all at once, the situation seemed to be comical of how she got out of dishes again and she began to giggle. If you ever heard her giggle, you would know how infectious it was. Before long we were both laughing until our sides were sore. Daddy didn't think it was funny at all. Now as a mother, I can see his side of it.

The year after Mom passed away, Dad bought a little pup home. He said we could name him. Being he was a tan colour, we named him Gopher.

Myself and Gopher

He grew up to be not very big. Helen and I both loved him. I think we gave the love to him that we would have given to Mom.

We lived in a low roofed two bedroom house that Dad built. It began as a one roomed shack but as more children arrived, Dad built it bigger. We had mice in our house. We always put out mouse traps at night which usually were occupied the next day. Our dog Gopher was a very good mouser. At night times, Helen and I would lie awake at night and listen to the "Mouse Olympics." They seemed to all be at one side and then all of a sudden they all ran across the ceiling at the same time. Then after a short time, they would all run back to the other side. This continued until we went to sleep.

For many years, there was an empty Flour Mill next door to our house. I don't ever remember it being occupied at any time. A year or two after Mom passed away, they decided to dismantle it. Dad knew there were probably many rats in this building and told us to make sure we kept all the doors tightly closed that day. The day they began tearing it down, John with our dog Gopher and Kathleen's son Charlie with his big black Labrador stood ready. As the rats ran out, the boys sent the dogs after them and they killed them one by one, in time to catch another rat. (This story still gives me the shivers.) I can't tell you how many rats there were but they lined them up in rows on a large garage door. The Saskatoon Star Phoenix printed a picture of the boys, the dogs and the dead rats. During this time, Helen and I and Bill's dog Louie were in the house with all the doors closed tightly. Bill and Corney were both at home so it must have been during the summer holidays. That night, John woke up and saw a rat climbing up the screen on the window in Dad's room. He got up and woke the other boys. Bill grabbed the 22 rifle. I heard a commotion and got up. The rat had left the window and was under the bed. Bill had the gun aimed ready to shoot. I told him he had to wake Dad up first. Dad had, what nowadays would be called sleep apnea. He snored VERY loudly and then would hold his breath what seemed to be forever and let his breath out with a loud burst of sound. I told Bill, he may as well shoot Dad, for a loud noise like that would probably give him a heart attack. I went back to our bedroom with Helen, Louie and Gopher and closed the door tight. By the time the boys got Dad got out of bed, the rat had disappeared. As they couldn't find it, they went back to bed. Helen and I endlessly kept calling out, "Are you positive it's not in here?" The answer was "No," each time we called out. We tried very hard not to go to sleep but finally sometime in the early morning we did fall asleep. Later in the morning when we got up, they told us that early in the morning, Corney woke up because of a nibbling on his toe. He shook Bill and started hitting him for biting him, before they both realized it was the rat. So they starting looking for it and found it under a cupboard that was on the opposite side of the wall at our heads. They shot it and we had been so tired from keeping ourselves awake for so long, that we never heard a sound. The first and last time we EVER had a rat in the house. Thank goodness!!

After Mom passed away, Helen and I didn't have birthday parties. We made parties for each other. Dad had a Canada Book in his bookcase. For my birthday Helen would wrap this book and give it to me. I would be so excited and thank her for such a wonderful gift! Then for her birthday (which was four days later) I would wrap the same book and give it to her. She would in turn be so excited and thank me for such a marvellous gift! Neither of us ever read the book. We did this for a couple years after Mom passed away. As I got older I would bake a cake for Helen. Once I was working in the Bank, I was able to give her nice gifts. As much as I missed Mom I couldn't help but think how much worse it was for Helen as she was three years younger than me.

Mrs McKechnie was one of our neighbours who lived behind our house in Aberdeen. She was known as Nana, not only to her grandchildren but also to most people in Aberdeen. Everyone loved her. She was a good cook and baker and she brought over many a good meal and delicious buns and cookies. Many of her grandchildren got to be very good friends of ours when they came to visit her. She was the mother of Eva Hamm, the wife of Eugene Hamm. Her house was a dream with four bedrooms and large living room and dining room. Her kitchen was small but big enough for her to be very busy in. The night before our wedding, myself and Carol Grieve (at that time,) slept in one of the bedrooms and Dad (Grandpa) and his best man Heinz Fedrau slept in another. At breakfast, she served Fruit Loops to all of us. This was in the very early days of Fruit Loops and after pouring milk on them the milk turned all kinds of colours. Not very appetizing looking but tasted good. So much for the old wives tale that the groom shouldn't see the bride the day of the wedding before the wedding ceremony. Dad (Grandpa) and I have been married almost sixty years as I am writing this.

As Nana advanced in age, she had the tendency to talk to herself. To see her walking through the back alley and busy talking when there was no one there, was usual.

Many years ago, her house was demolished and replaced with a new house. Her house was one of the houses I dreamed of living in some day.

The other house I dreamed of many times was the home of two of our school friends. This large two story house was across the train tracks on the south east corner of Aberdeen. It also had a very large barn on the yard. The house was surrounded on three sides with a large deck. On the north side the deck was enclosed with screens. Sometimes on a hot summer day when we stayed there for night, the four of us slept out there. The rooms inside seemed huge to us. Nowadays they probably wouldn't seem that big at all. There was a very wide wooden staircase leading upstairs. The girl's bedroom was very large. One wall was built in cupboards in which there was a space for their child sized table and chairs. We thought they had to be the luckiest two girls in the whole world.

The house had to be demolished some years ago as the racoons got into the attic and destroyed the inside. When Brendan and Leslee told us about the house they were building, and then showed us pictures of the house, it sounded like and looked just like that house. When we went to Brendan and Leslee's for the first time after it was built, I had to hold back tears. It was the dream house of my childhood but on a smaller scale.

I babysat as often as I could when I was in high school,. The first thing I bought was a navy blazer and a pair of blue jeans. Grandpa would never give us money to buy jeans. In fact he never thought I needed clothes at all. Some well meaning? lady in town gave me a big box of dresses. There were navy dresses, black dresses, dark green dresses and brown dresses. To me they were old lady dresses. I'm sure she got rid of all her old dresses so she could buy new bright and colourful dresses. I did have to wear one once when Lydia was home.

Speaking of clothes, I must tell you about our "magic washing machine." Neither Helen and me or even Dad knew much about sorting clothes before washing them. Helen and me each had a pale blue jersey blouse. Each time we washed those blouses they came out a different colour. They were pink, navy, purple, lavender, and blue. Our friends in school thought we were so lucky to have so many pretty blouses. We never said a word about our "magic washing machine,"or else we would be doing their wash, too.

Water for washing clothes came from the dugout in the summer and in the winter, Dad melted snow on the stove. Same with our weekly bath. We did only bathe once a week as it was a lot of work to heat the water on the stove. Helen bathed first, then I, then John, (when he was at home) and lastly Dad. During the week, I often washed my Dad's feet and clipped his toenails.

In the summertime, in those days, we would play outside with our friends until well after dark. Helen and I rode our bikes during the day time. The agent for the National Grain Elevator lived behind our house. When the elevator wasn't busy he would let Helen and I walk our bikes up the ramp leading in and ride down the ramp. In the evening we played around the grain cars on the tracks near the station. We probably shouldn't have done that, but either no one ever saw us, or if they did, they didn't care. We never had to lock our doors. In those days, everyone left their doors unlocked as we trusted everyone. In winter we often had large snow banks and we loved rolling down the banks. Skating was another thing we enjoyed. We never had the chance to learn to figure skate as there never was anyone in Aberdeen that could teach it.

I babysat a lot in town. I got along good with little ones and never had a problem. One day, a lady who lived on a farm north of town with her husband, came and asked if I would come there for a couple of days to pick and shell peas. Of course I went. When we got there she took me upstairs and showed me my room. It was simple but beautiful! I had a bed all to myself! I knew how Anne of Green Gables must have felt when she moved to Green Gables, but in reality I was still Annie of the Village. I wasn't an orphan (thank goodness) and I only slept there two nights.

As well as our girlfriends, we had two other good friends, Melvin and Bobby. We had a lot of fun together. We had a big shock one day. I was working in the bank at the time and the others were all still in school. Your Dad (Grandpa) had come down to see me for the weekend. We took Helen into Saskatoon to see a show. After that we drove back to Aberdeen. As we needed a loaf of bread, we stopped at the store and Helen went in. Before long Helen came out, without the bread and got into the truck. I asked her how come she didn't get the bread. She said, "Melvin is dead." I couldn't believe her but she said he and Bobby had been in a car accident and Melvin was dead. We found out the details later. Melvin had been driving too fast and as they came to the top of a hill, he lost control and they ended upside down in a slough. Melvin didn't make it but they got Bobby out. The hospital spent a lot of time working on Bobby and he did pull through. The ironic thing was that Bobby (who was an epileptic) went to Ontario to visit his brother later in the summer. He was standing on the edge of a dock at a lake, had an epileptic attack, fell in and drowned.

Losing Melvin put Helen into shock. Dad and I were very worried. She wouldn't talk, she wouldn't eat and seemed to be in a real trance. The night before Melvin's funeral, I had a dream that Melvin hadn't been killed but his brother Ken had. Us girls were walking down the street crying and Melvin came along and said, "You know Ken wouldn't want you crying." I woke up and it was as if Melvin sent a message to me. Of course, Melvin wouldn't want us to cry over him. The funeral was a sad day but after that Helen seem to settle down and we all pulled together to help each other.

Helen and I had "town"girlfriends and then there were our "country"girlfriends. After we were married we lost track of our "town" girlfriends except for a couple of them. The "country" girlfriends are still and no doubt will be my dearest friends for the rest of my life.

The summer after Mom passed away, I began to get migraine headaches. My headaches would start with bright zig zags and then shortly after that I would begin to see blank spaces. Then an intense headache would follow. If I started to get one of these headaches in school, I would go tell the teacher that I was going home as I was getting a headache. Some of the teachers were very ignorant about this. I had no choice as I had to get home while I could still see. I never argued or even felt intimidated by them. I left school as fast as I could and got home as quickly as possible. Once home I pulled the curtains and got into bed. Dad really didn't want to give me aspirins as they said that Mom had taken so many aspirins for her head-aches that it thinned out her blood so much they couldn't help her at the last. Tylenol had not yet been discovered in those days. So I waited out the headache. I was okay by the next day. My migraines continued through the years until I was over sixty.

CGIT was an important part of Helen and my life. Kathleen Gordon was the leader and we loved her dearly. She would have the meetings at her house. She did not have a very large house and it certainly was disorderly. That didn't bother us at all. We learned how to quilt and when we were doing this, she set down the rules that young ladies should mind. I remember one of the questions was, "If a boy gets fresh with me, what should I do?" Her answer was "Take your hand, hold it back as far as you can, and then bring it forward as fast as you can and make contact with his cheek." Such sound advice! Kathleen was the mother Helen and I didn't have anymore.

When I was 15 years old, I attended CGIT Camp at Regina Beach. I took the bus from Aberdeen to Saskatoon and then I transferred to another bus to Regina. I arrived in Regina and began looking for my luggage. They were nowhere to be found. After phoning to the Bus Depot in Saskatoon, I found out my luggage was still sitting in Saskatoon. I thought they would automatically transfer my luggage to the Regina bus. Not so. So for the first day or so, I was at the mercy of the girls in my cabin. Thank goodness they weren't all as nasty as the one girl. The others shared clothes, pyjamas, tooth paste, comb and bedding with me. What a relief when my luggage arrived. I really enjoyed camp. We did a lot of singing, which I loved the most. I made a lot of friends, especially when they didn't have to share their things with me. The leaders were very good and we had so much fun.

At sixteen, I graduated from CGIT in a ceremony held in Saskatoon.

My CGIT Graduation

So much fun and so many good memories!

CHAPTER 14
More Memories

More of my childhood memories keep creeping back into my mind. Some of these are:

- walking along the railroad tracks to our friends place, two miles west of Aberdeen. There weren't many trains in those days and I don't recall ever having to step off the tracks for one. The trains at that time were pulled by steam engines and were not near as fast as the trains are these days. Also, train traffic was not very heavy then.

- picking wild strawberries in the ditches beside the railroad track. They were more delicious than any strawberries you can buy nowadays.

- swimming on a hot day in a little pond on a friends farm just out of town. We couldn't swim but it sounds better than just saying we played in the water.

- going to visit an Aunt who lived in an apartment in Saskatoon. Wow! We thought she had to be the richest person in the world to be able to live in an apartment. What a fantasy!

- the Church Board asking Helen and I to do the cleaning at the church so we would have a little money of our own. We didn't do it for too long. The work of dusting the pews and cleaning the rug wasn't bad. But going into the basement, knowing our mother's casket had been there, was almost more than we could handle. I remember well, us slamming the basement door shut and running up the steps in a cold sweat, sure there was a ghost behind us.

- riding our bikes to Vonda with our friends and then phoning our friend's Dad to come and pick us up as we were too tired to ride back. Vonda was nine miles away.

- taking the train to Vonda to visit friends on a Saturday morning and almost missing the train back in the evening. Especially when there wasn't any passenger trains on Sunday and we hadn't told Dad where we were going.

- Helen's trick of going to the outside toilet in the summer and reading the Eaton's catalogue until dishes were done.

- going out on Halloween but not pulling pranks like our brothers. There was a man in town that made our brothers' lives miserable more times than once. They went to his place, and tipped over his outside toilet on the door, not knowing he was waiting inside the toilet to catch them.

- my nickname in my teenage years was Skinflint. I was very skinny. In CGIT we had to wear a middy which had a large v-neck. My friends said I should put safety pins in my ear lobes and attach them to the collar of my middy so it wouldn't fall down. Those days have long ago been left in the past.

- something that our friends and Helen and I would do was to buy a large Spanish onion. Slice it and put it in vinegar. The next day we would eat it and do up another onion for the following day. I don't recall how long this went on but we did notice that nobody wanted to come near us.

- Helen teasing me about my flat nose and I told her I would rather have a flat nose than a ski jump like hers. Sisterly love!!

- when spring was on it's way, the snow would melt first on the south side of the house. Helen and I loved to go there and play in the warm soil. It smelled so good, too.

- a friend loaned me her piano accordion which I also learned to play.

- once, when Dad came back from visiting his brother Abe and family at Swift Current, he brought Helen and I each a watch. It was the first time Helen and I had ever had a watch. Boy did we feel good when we went to school to show off our watches. Almost everyone already had watches but that didn't dampen our excitement.

- Sports Day was a big event in Aberdeen. One year during the Sports Day, a thunder and lightening storm came up suddenly. I quickly ran home. My brother John and a friend of his were there already. Just as I came in, there was a loud rumble of thunder and a knot fell out of a hole in the ceiling in the porch. I stepped into the house to tell the boys about it, when there was a huge crack of lightning and the radio fell to the floor with sparks flying. I didn't know what happened until John started screaming. He had been disconnecting the wires to the radio from the outside antenna when lightning struck the outside antenna pole, as he had both hands on the two wires. John was dancing around. He took his shoe off and his big toe was black. He quickly put his shoe on and ran to the hardware store to get a window pane to replace the broken window pane. He was so worried that Dad would be upset with him for breaking the window. He was just about finished putting it in when Dad came home. He had heard at the Sports Ground that our house had been hit with lightning. Dad was just glad we were all well.

CHAPTER 15
Growing Up, a Little

When I graduated from School, I wanted to be a Psychiatric Nurse at Essendale, B.C. Two girls from Aberdeen were nurses there and they said they would help me out. A close family friend said he would lend me the money to go there. After applying, I received a letter saying the course started on August 25 and I wasn't of age until August 30. They said I could go there and work in the hospital until the next training session started. I cried and cried. I knew I wasn't going anywhere. After all, why was I so selfish to think that I could leave Dad and Helen.

Unknown to me, Dad went and talked to the Bank Manager. He called me in and offered me a job. Of course I said yes. I wasn't too happy at the time although I did really enjoy working in the bank. I believe God has a plan for all of us, if we listen. If I had moved from Aberdeen, I may never have met your Dad (Grandpa) and for that I will always be thankful to the Lord.

I didn't date much but I dated a boy from a near by town twice. The first and the last! One late fall evening when he brought me home, Dad was outside trying to move a barrel that had a few inches of ice in it. As he was moving it, he dropped it on his foot. This young lad jumped out of the car to help him but he just turned around and stomped away. I am positive that Dad broke his foot that night but he sure wasn't going to let any young "whipper snipper" help him. That boy never came around again.

One of my best friends, after graduating from high school was Bernice Miner. Bernice was a school teacher and the two of us got along very well. She boarded at the bank manager and his wife's house. Many Saturday's we took the early bus to Saskatoon, shopped all day, and then returned home on the later bus. After leaving Aberdeen, Bernice took a teaching job at Inuvik, North West Territories. Her letters were of great interest as she could vividly describe her life up there. Bernice ended up marrying a farmer at Hanley. She has passed away since.

Wages were not great when I worked in the bank. At the time we got married, I was clearing one hundred dollars a month. Though I didn't pay rent, I bought curtains for the windows, bought paint and painted the walls inside. Many a time I bought groceries. I also bought myself nice clothes and before getting married I bought a full length genuine mouton fur coat for one hundred dollars. As the only money Helen made was from babysitting, I bought her some nice clothes too. Dad's suit was pretty shabby so I bought him a brand new suit, shirt and tie. Also there were only a few TV's around so I bought Dad a brand new TV. On Saturday evening Dad's friends would come down to watch wrestling. It was worth your life to walk into the living room while they were watching as fists were flying. I am surprised that one of them didn't get hit.

In the summer of 1956, Helen and I went to the wedding of a friend. While there, we met Hilda and Heinz Fedrau. We hit it off very well so when two weeks later, I saw Heinz's car driving around town, I told Helen that we had to go to the cafe for a coke. As we walked into the cafe Heinz and this reddish haired, red faced, white eyebrow guy was sitting together. We walked up and innocently said, "What a surprise! What are you doing in town?" So the four of us chatted and then went for a car ride around town. Heinz's friend, Fred, had a red face from working outside in the summer heat and his eyebrows were white as a reaction to kerosene lanterns used for lighting in the house. When they left that evening, I knew in my heart that I had met the one I wanted to spend the rest of my life with.

The next week I had holidays so I took a trip to British Columbia to visit Grandpa and Grandma and my Aunts. This was the year before your Dad (Grandpa) and I were married. I took the train "The Canadian" out of Saskatoon to Vancouver. I went to Saskatoon by bus in the middle of July 1956. It had rained heavy in Saskatoon. So I walked from the bus depot to the train station. I was wearing a white dress with little stars on it, white high heeled shoes and a green tweed summer coat. On the way to the station, while crossing a street, I stepped into what I thought was a puddle, but was a pot hole. In I went well past my ankles. My shoes were soaked, the bottom of my dress and coat were soaked. I thought I had looked pretty good but I ended up looking like a drowned out tramp. Puts a new meaning to the saying "Pride goeth before the fall." First thing I did when I got to the station was change my clothes. My wet clothes were in my suitcase until I got to Aunt Helen's in Vancouver. At least I had enough sense to take my suitcases with me and not expect them to automatically transfer them to the train.

I was so glad I had come to British Columbia. What a beautiful country! I was so glad to see Grandma and Grandpa.

Grandma and Grandpa Matthies

They lived at Sardis where they had a cute little farm. Uncle Abe, whom I really liked, lived with them. My Aunt Katie (Mom's brother John's wife) and her family lived next door. Cousin Lottie and I hit it off right away. One evening Cousin Corney took Lottie and I to a nearby resort, Cultis Lake. I had never roller skated before or again but I did that night. We had a ball! Lottie was so much fun. After we finished roller skating, we needed to go to the washroom. We found a long building that said "Women" on the outside. There was no power in it. So I went to the first stall and Lottie went farther down. I felt around and found a what seemed to be a barrel. "What a poor set up for such a nice resort," I thought. Oh well! I perched on the edge and started relieving myself. It was quite a drumming sound. "What are you doing?" asked Lottie. "The same as you." I replied. When done I felt around and found a sink. I was washing my hands as Lottie came up. I told her what I thought of their poor facilities. Lottie felt around and told me I had just gone in the barrel for used towels. The toilets were farther down. We laughed all the way back to Sardis. Corney was getting quite upset with us but we just couldn't stop laughing.

The next day Uncle Abe took me to Vancouver where I visited with Aunt Helen and Uncle John. After spending a couple of nights with them, I walked to my Aunt Katheryne's. While I was walking, I walked by a high metal fence with a police dog sitting by the house. Being used to a small town where you talked to and petted everyone's dogs, I started talking to him as I was walking. Suddenly he let out a ferocious growl and lunged to the fence. I was no longer walking. I was running as fast as I could. I have been cautious about dogs ever since.

While at Aunt Helen's they took me to Stanley Park and to Capilano Canyon. Uncle John was a scarey driver but we never had an accident. At Capilano Canyon we walked on the swinging bridge. In a souvenir shop I bought a small replica of the Capilano wishing well. Aunt Helen taped a penny in the well and told me to make a wish. She said if my wish comes true I could take the penny out. After Dad (Grandpa) and I were married, I took the penny out as that was the wish I had made.

Myself at Capilano Canyon in British Columbia

On the way home, I stopped off in Calgary and had a great visit with my brother Corney and his wife Gladys.

I really enjoyed my visit to British Columbia and also enjoyed travelling on the train.

On November 18, 1956, your Dad (Grandpa) was driving me home from Central Butte, where I spent the weekend visiting with his family. On the way home, he pulled of the road, shut the truck off, and proposed to me. Of course I said yes. After all I knew this was what I wanted since I had first met him. Your Dad (Grandpa) and I were married in the Mennonite Church in Aberdeen on July 6, 1957.

Fred and my wedding day

When your Dad (Grandpa) and I were married, we left town on the north road to go to Cochin Lake for our honeymoon. When we came back, Helen told us that, each day, until we came back from our honeymoon, Gopher would go about a block away from home, on the same road as we took when we left town, and sit at the side of the road. He just sat there looking down the road. She had to pick him up and carry him home to eat and for night. As the soon as the door opened again, he was back in the same place, waiting for us to come back. After we came back and left for Central Butte, he didn't bother again.

When Helen got married and left town, Gopher just got weaker and weaker every day, until the day he passed away. Dad said he died of a broken heart, (made us feel real good - NOT). He wouldn't tell us where he buried him but Helen and I were both sure that he buried him under the big apple tree.

As I have written this story to my family, I failed to mention who my family are. They are: our son Dale (Kathy); our daughters Kathy (Garry Schaan); Judy (Roger Galenza); Donna Brown; Wendy (Michael Thienes); our grandsons, Brendan (Leslee) Brown; Aaron (Rachel Min) Brown; Curtis Schaan; Logan Thienes; our granddaughters, Trisha Schaan (Curtis Hanson); Auburn Thienes; our great grandchildren Avery and Colter Brown; our extended family, Lana (Brent Watts), daughters Haley and Brynn; Brian (Corinne) O'Neill and children Maeryn, Brody and Teagan

Epilogue

Besides my Dad, there are some other people that I need to mention that have helped to shape my life. I feel these people have been written on my heart."

****

My little sister Helen was certainly deeply written on my heart. I never felt alone growing up because Helen was always there. We fought a lot as sisters do, but we wouldn't allow anyone be unkind to each other. We laughed together a lot. And when needed, we hugged each other and cried together.

One of those times was when Helen got her first period. When she told me, we both hugged and cried together. No one had ever told me about that either and I was helpless to help her. I know Helen was scared. Oh how we missed our Mom that day. I remember Mom attempting to tell me the facts of life but she was very sick at the time and couldn't talk long. Helen and I had other such moments when the loneliness for our Mom got the best of us. We spent most of our time being brave for Dad but there were other times we just couldn't do it and we hugged each other and cried. I still miss her very much and still shed tears for her even if it has been fifteen years since she passed away.

One day after we were married, Helen and Frank and their family came to visit. Helen and I were talking about Mom and I told her the only thing I had to remember her by, was a black babushka (shawl) that had belonged to her mother. Helen said she didn't even have that much. I excused myself and left the room. I took a pair of scissors and cut it in half. I went back in the room and gave her one of the halves. I told her, "Now you have as much as I do."

****

Kathleen Gordon, my second mother. Helen and I got to know Kathleen when she taught CGIT. Canadian Girls In Training was a interdenominational group of teen aged girls. We learned to make quilts, which we did at Kathleen's house. As we quilted we had discussions from boys to religion to everyday events. She was someone we could go to when we had a problem, She always seemed to find time for us. As Helen and I didn't have a mom anymore, she was someone we really treasured. Dad (Grandpa) and I named our first daughter after her. We kept up our friendship with Kathleen through the years right up to her passing at a home in Calgary at the age of one hundred and two.

There are many women who are proud to have had Kathleen in their life. I am one of them. She was the one whose shoulder I could cry on and who I got hugs from when I needed a mother's touch. We will meet again, Kathleen.

****

Ike Thiessen, my former choir director was a great man in my eyes. He was a fabulous choir director who made us work hard but it was always fun. Some of our anthems were sung in German. He was very patient with me as I stumbled through learning the German pronunciation. He always picked such good songs to sing. We had practice on Wednesday evenings. I didn't miss once, even when I wouldn't be there on Sunday. My friends couldn't understand why I would bother going if I wouldn't be there on Sunday. I couldn't understand why they would even ask me that because I enjoyed music so much.

As I have been successful in leading senior and junior choirs and glee clubs, and teaching three of my girls to sing three part harmony, I owe my music ability and also my great love of music to Ike. Thanks to you, Ike. Rest in peace.

****

Eugene Hamm, the School Principal. Eugene was the principal of Aberdeen most of the years I went to school. He taught Algebra, Art History and I don't remember what other subjects because those two were the ones I loved most. After we were married, when we went to Aberdeen, we made it a point to visit Eugene and his wife Eva. On one of these visits, I mentioned to him that my flat nose really bothered me. He asked why. I told him a girl in one of the earlier classes in school used to tease me terribly about my flat nose. Always in front of the other children. I know many times this made me cry. Eugene asked if I knew why she was teased me so badly about my nose. I said I didn't know. He asked what there was about her that wasn't perfect. I said she had a speech defect. Then he told me that she teased me so that the kids wouldn't tease her about her speech. Eugene then turned sideways and said, "Have you ever looked at my nose?" Well no, I certainly never had. His nose was HUGE. I never noticed that before. So the mystery of that girl's teasing was solved.

Eugene not only had been my favourite teacher but also taught me to look at life at more ways than one. He was a very positive influence in my life, while I was in school and after I had graduated.

You will never be forgotten, Eugene.

****

I hope you all enjoy reading about my childhood as much as I enjoyed reliving the many memories that I have and can still remember. To my family, I leave you this book as my legacy.

"Being a family does not mean you are linked by blood, but it does mean you will love and will be loved for the rest of your life. No matter what."

CPSIA information can be obtained
at www.ICGtesting.com
Printed in the USA
LVHW01s0435170518
577322LV00005B/87/P